The Ultimate Motorcycles

SCOOTERS

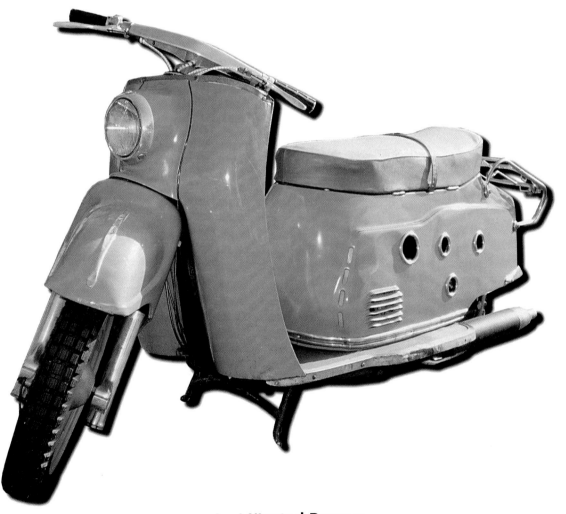

Lori Kinstad Pupeza
ABDO Publishing Company

visit us at
www.abdopub.com

Published by Abdo Publishing Company 4940 Viking Drive, Edina, Minnesota 55435.
Copyright © 1998 by Abdo Consulting Group, Inc. International copyrights reserved in all
countries. No part of this book may be reproduced in any form without written permission
from the publisher.

Printed in the United States.

Photo credits: Michael Dregni, Eric Dregni, Jeremy Herridge, Honda, AP/Wide World

Edited by Kal Gronvall

Library of Congress Cataloging-in-Publication Data

Pupeza, Lori Kinstad
    Scooters / Lori Kinstad Pupeza.
        p. cm. -- (The ultimate motorcycles)
  Includes index.
  Summary: Discusses the development of the motor scooter, its popularity during the
depression and its uses in wartime, as well as its disadvantages in a world much
concerned with pollution
   ISBN 1-57765-003-4
   1. Motor scooters--History--Juvenile literature.   [1.Motor scooters] I. Title. II. Series:
Pupeza, Lori Kinstad. Ultimate motorcycle series
TL450.P86 1998
629.227'5--dc21

                        97-53098
                        CIP
                        AC

Warning: The series *The Ultimate Motorcycles* is intended as entertainment for
children. These activities should never be attempted without training, instruction,
supervision, and proper equipment.

Contents

Scooters

No other word describes scooters better than fun. The cheerful little machines can put a smile on anybody's face. They are affectionately nicknamed "putt-putts" by their owners. They've been around since cars and motorcycles, and people continue to drive them all over the world. History has proven that their popularity can't be smothered. People also love them for their practicality. They have survived because they get good gas mileage, and because people feel happy riding them.

Throughout the 1900s, the scooter and the motorcycle were at opposite ends of the spectrum. The motorcycle represents a greasy kind of toughness, with images like black leather jackets. The scooter represents all things good and wholesome—like ironed shirts and fluffy kitties. People riding scooters look like they're out on a fun adventure.

Throughout history the scooter was popular for different reasons. After the Depression, they were economical to drive. In the 1960s, they were considered cool. In some countries scooters were a necessity. In the 1990s, developing countries and densely populated countries use them to get around easier and faster. No matter where a person goes, scooters are always popular.

American teenagers look forward to turning 15 so they can finally have their own transportation, even if it is only a scooter or a moped. Early inventors couldn't have guessed the size of the impact that scooters have made in the world.

The Honda Elite.

Early Scooters

The early 1900s were a fascinating time. Speed was a new thing. Cars and motorcycles were built with a new invention, the internal combustion engine. "Fast" was something that most people had only experienced on a horse or a train. It wasn't long before everybody wanted a taste of speed.

Some people wanted a car. Others thought motorcycles were better. Then there were those people who just wanted something to get them around town to run errands or visit friends. The invention of the motorscooter filled the need for a runabout vehicle.

The history of the motorscooter began in the United States, and parts of Europe during the 1910s and 1920s. Some of these first scooters looked like a child's push scooter with an engine attached to either the front or back wheel. They didn't have brakes. To stop, a person had to put their foot down on the ground. These early scooters couldn't go very fast. Most couldn't go over 20 mph (32 kmph).

The engine was sometimes mounted to the left side of the wheel, which made the scooter unbalanced. In addition, the handlebars were attached to an almost vertical steering spindle, making it very easy to take too sharp of a turn and fall on the ground.

During the 1920s, the scooter, then called the Autoped or Motoped, was more of a play thing than a serious form of transportation. They were sold primarily for ladies to run around town. They had a step-through frame that allowed room for all the layers of ruffles and petticoats that women wore in those days.

Unfortunately the scooter craze ended as quickly as it began. In 1935, a magazine called the *Motor Cycle* said of the early scooters that "They vibrated to an extent that was almost unbelievable and their reliability was far from high, and they were not exactly comfortable with their small-diameter wheels and small-section tyres [tires]. The scooter was killed—by the scooter."

Scooters have kept their basic design over the years.

The Great Depression

At the end of the 1920s, the Great Depression hit America. People didn't have money for expensive transportation, like cars. Two men named E. Foster Salsbury and Austin Elmore had an idea about a vehicle that people could afford. Salsbury saw the aviator Amelia Earhart riding a scooter around an airport one day, and he realized that he could manufacture scooters. Thus began the second craze of the scooter. People had a real need for scooters and had forgotten how awful they were almost 10 years before. Salsbury's timing couldn't have been better.

Salsbury eventually played a part in the Cushman motorscooter company. He also played a part in the Moto-Scoot, the Mead Ranger, the Powell, the Rock-Ola, the Crocker Scootabout, the Keen Power Cycle, the Puddlejumper, and many others. This new generation of putt-putts were better built machines. They had brakes and transmissions. They were better styled. The engines were covered in body work. Fenders covered the previously open tires. Engines sputtered less often. Scooters could scoot down the road at 30 mph (48 kmph).

In 1937, the Motor Glide, built by E. Foster Salsbury and Austin Elmore, was plush and comfortable to ride. Electric features like a horn, headlights, and tail lamp were supplied with power from six

6-volt batteries. Although there wasn't any suspension, a well cushioned seat provided plenty of give down bumpy roads. It wasn't until 1939 that the Motor-Glide came equipped with a fully automatic transmission.

Also in 1937, the Cushman Motor Works company came out with the Auto-glide. It also had electrical devices and boasted of easy handling. The company advertised the Cushman scooter as the "genuine American Thrill!" Cushman built engines, and the motorscooter was just another way for the company to sell their engines. Cushman eventually became the longest-lived scooter company ever.

Scooters became popular again during the Great Depression because they were economical to drive.

The scooter designed by Salsbury and Elmore was used as a template for all scooters to come. Their scooters always had five things: a step-through chassis, bodywork to keep the driver from getting dirty, a small motor next to or in front of the back wheel, small wheels, and an automatic transmission/clutch. All scooters that came after the 1937 Motor-Glide had at least three of these five features.

The late 1930's were a time of pinching pennies and not wasting anything. Coming out of a depression and heading into a World War, the scooter became a substitute for the more expensive car. The Cushman's Auto-Glide was advertised as getting over 120 miles (193 km) to the gallon. A tank of gas would go a long way, and operating costs weren't much either.

Manufacturers even made build-it-yourself scooters for those who couldn't afford an already-assembled scooter. The LeJay Manufacturing Company even offered plans (for only 25 cents) to build an electric scooter. The scooter, called the Electric Rocket, couldn't go very fast and had no transmission or clutch. The first scooters invented during the 1910s and 1920s didn't last because they were considered frivolous toys for adults. The reinvented scooters of the late 1930s lasted because they were inexpensive, practical, and in some cases, the only transportation people could afford at that time.

The Depression made scooters more practical to drive.

Putt-Putts and Parachutes

During World War II, from 1939 to 1945, scooters played a different role. Scooters became a secret weapon of sorts, used by America, Italy, Great Britain, and possibly others. Scooters were built small enough to fold up and be carried. Soldiers who parachuted to the ground, called paratroopers, were dropped behind enemy lines carrying the tiny machines. When they hit the ground, they unpacked their scooters, and could quickly move to attack enemy soldiers.

Cushman motorscooters were used the most by American soldiers. They were tested by tying a rope to the scooter, tossing the rope over a tree branch, pulling the scooter up in the air, and dropping it. When it didn't break, they sent it off to be used in the war. Because the scooters were dropped from high above, they weren't equipped with headlights. The glass might have broken, and just added on more weight. Suspension and engine covers also weren't used. They were considered luxury items, and making the scooters as light as possible was the most important thing. The 1944 Cushman Model 53 Airborne Scooter weighed 255 pounds (115 kg)!

Scooters were more laughable than effective in many situations. The scooters were probably the worst killing machines that the military ever used. The two-stroke engines were loud and smoky. They were slow and clumsy. They made better targets than transports. France made the ACMA Vespa Military Scooter that was thankfully never put into combat. It was loaded with bazookas that, if ever fired, would probably do more damage to the scooter than to the enemy. The force of shooting bazookas would probably flip a scooter over and destroy it.

During the war back in America, scooters were still in production. During a time when car production ceased, the Cushman Scooter company was manufacturing 300 scooters a day. Scooters were still in demand in America. Companies wondered what a postwar world wanted. The answer was anything new and different. New designs and new manufacturers popped up in Japan, France, and Italy.

The Lambretta fold up paratrooper scooter was used by the military.

The Parts of a Scooter

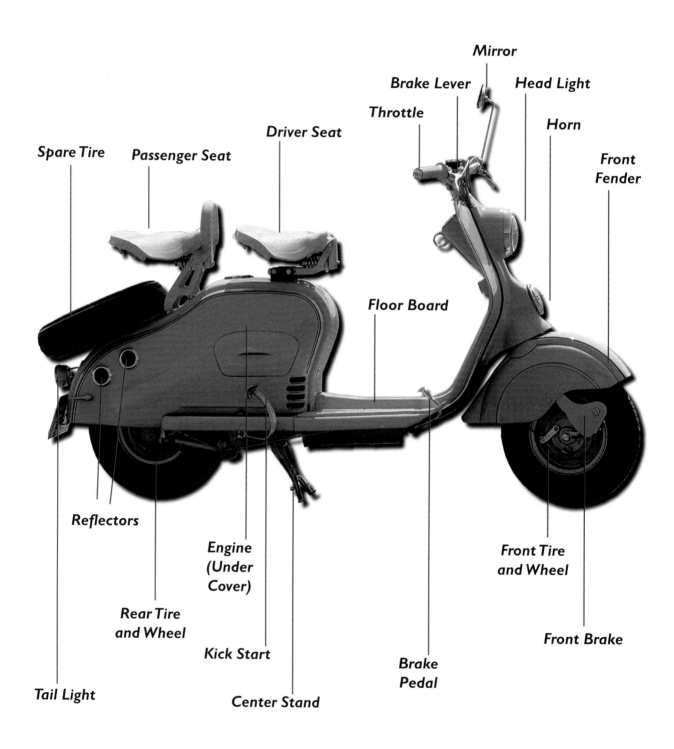

Mirror

Brake Lever

Head Light

Throttle

Horn

Driver Seat

Front Fender

Spare Tire

Passenger Seat

Floor Board

Reflectors

Engine (Under Cover)

Front Tire and Wheel

Rear Tire and Wheel

Kick Start

Front Brake

Tail Light

Brake Pedal

Center Stand

How a Two-Stroke Engine Works

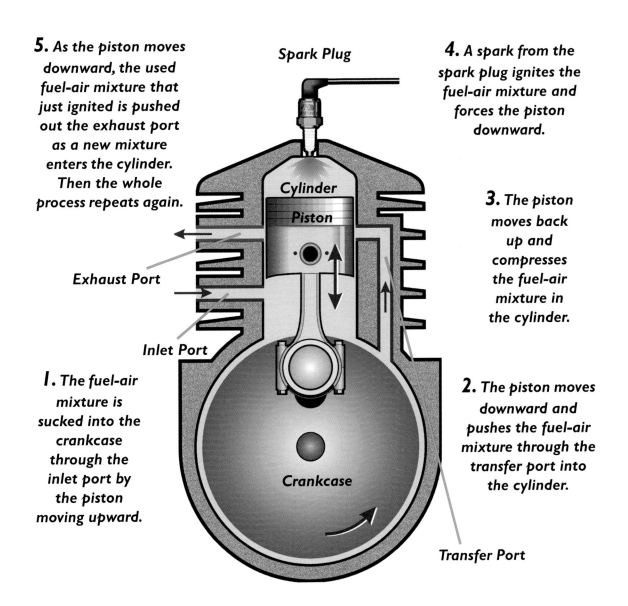

5. *As the piston moves downward, the used fuel-air mixture that just ignited is pushed out the exhaust port as a new mixture enters the cylinder. Then the whole process repeats again.*

Spark Plug

4. *A spark from the spark plug ignites the fuel-air mixture and forces the piston downward.*

Cylinder

Piston

3. *The piston moves back up and compresses the fuel-air mixture in the cylinder.*

Exhaust Port

Inlet Port

1. *The fuel-air mixture is sucked into the crankcase through the inlet port by the piston moving upward.*

2. *The piston moves downward and pushes the fuel-air mixture through the transfer port into the cylinder.*

Crankcase

Transfer Port

The Vespa and the Lambretta

One of the most popular types of scooter was developed in the postwar era. In 1946, the Piaggio Company began production of the Vespa. The scooter was named Vespa because the two-stroke engine made a buzzing sound like a wasp. Vespa is the Italian word for wasp. The company produced 2,484 scooters the first year. In its second year, in 1947, production jumped to 10,535 scooters. In 1994, over 10 million Vespas were made. The word scooter has become interchangeable with Vespa.

People loved the design of a Vespa. During the 1950s, Piaggio improved the scooter. It had controls on the handlebars that made it easier to drive, and attractive styling. The saddle seat, which fit two riders on a scooter, made riding a scooter a social occasion. The Vespa had durable tires to avoid the roadside flat, and was easy to steer and handle. The refined, beautiful machine behaved as gracefully as it looked.

The design of the Vespa came from the mind of an aviator and engineer, which was evident by the sheet-metal and strong frame. A new scooter, called the Lambretta, was built by a plumber. The frame was made out of pipes. Ferdinando Innocenti, another Italian, wanted to build a scooter that anybody could afford. The name Lambretta came from the factory's site that sat next to the

Lambro River, near Milan, Italy. The Lambretta and the Vespa scooters began a rivalry with each other, trying to build a faster, more reliable, more beautiful machine year after year.

The Lambretta filled a niche in war-ravaged Italy. It was a less expensive vehicle, and looked more like a motorcycle than the Vespa. It had a big open engine and a tube chassis. The scooter carried a 125 cc engine, which was more powerful than Vespa's 98 cc engine.

The Lambretta could go faster (44 mph, or 71 kmph) than the Vespa (only 35 mph, or 56 kmph). This pushed Vespa to keep up with Lambretta's superior engine, and Lambretta to keep its driver dry and clean with bodywork like the Vespa. Lots of other companies built scooters in the late 1940s and early 1950s, but nobody did it as well as these two companies.

The Vespa is one of the most popular scooters ever made.

Scooters also filled Japan's need for cheap transportation. The company named Fuji built one of Japan's favorite motorscooters— the Rabbit. Not long after, Mitsubishi built a scooter called the Pigeon. They looked like the postwar American versions of scooters, and they ruled the far-eastern market from the late 1940s to the 1960s.

A small company at that time, Honda, produced its first scooter in 1954. The styling was different from its competitors. The body design was much more advanced compared to the other scooters of the time. Each scooter company had its own styling. England and Germany had their own models too.

The 1964 Mitsubishi Silver Pigeon.

This is an advertisement for the
1947 Lambretta scooter.

Lambretta

The Scooter Effect

Advertisements for the scooters told stories about postwar culture. People wanted to have fun, and many advertisements showed women driving scooters. Not only did this make a scooter look fun and attractive, but it also gave the appearance of freedom and mobility.

Independence was something for which women were fighting. Women were told in the advertisements that a scooter was just as much an accessory as lipstick and earrings. The kind of people who bought scooters were men and women who wanted inexpensive transportation without having to get dirty. Scooter owners wanted to ride to work in their suits and ties and go grocery shopping in dresses and high heels.

These kind of people also didn't change the oil or tune up the engine on their scooters. As a result, engines were worn out, pushed to their limits, and died an early death. Owners soon learned that they needed to take care of their scooters. This started a need for service mechanics, and a lot of young people who were just learning about engines worked on beat-up, neglected, oil-spraying, exhaust-spewing, run-down scooters.

Because they were so inexpensively made, they broke down a lot. Almost every scooter owner had at least one story about scooter parts falling off and clanking down the road behind them. Owners came to expect not always reaching their destination—at least not without some minor problem. If there would have been product liability laws in those days, scooter companies probably would have gone bankrupt from lawsuits.

Despite all the problems with scooters, they remained a part of culture all over the world. In the movie *Roman Holiday*, actors Audrey Hepburn and Gregory Peck fell in love while riding around on a Vespa. A drive on a scooter was made out to be as romantic as a ride in a horse drawn carriage. In 1957, *Popular Science* magazine wrote that "Sports riders in this country are mostly either single or newly married (scooters are so conducive to romance that there is a fast turnover between these categories)."

An advertisement for the 1961 Mitsubishi Silver Pigeon Gale Pet.

The Mods and the Rockers

The scooter's popularity kept mounting during the late 1950s. Outrageous advertisements and scooter driving schools only added fuel to the fire. Travel agencies were booking scooter getaways. For a small amount of money, a person could rent a cabin on the beach and a couple of scooters to get there with.

By the time 1960 rolled around, having a scooter was just part of being hip. The world was changing, and in England, young people who drove scooters were called the Mods. The Mods were into American pop music, weird hairdos, and Lambretta or Vespa Scooters. Those who were considered Mods customized their scooters by adding lots of chrome, mirrors, and headlights.

The Mods' rival group was called the Rockers. The Rockers drove motorcycles, wore leather jackets, and slicked back their hair. The Rockers were more wild than the civilized Mods.

The Rockers would hang out at coffee shops listening to music on juke boxes. They would hop on their café racers (a type of motorcycle) as soon as a song started and try to get around the block before the song ended.

There was even a movie about the Mods and the Rockers, named *Quadrophenia*. The movie was about a real riot that broke out between the two groups. The scooter company Innocenti wanted to sponsor a scooter show on the beaches in Brighton, England. The Rockers found out about it and showed up at the show also. It didn't take long before the two crowds started scuffling, and violence erupted. Not long after that riot the two groups ended.

A scene from the movie **Quadrophenia** *that profiled the Mods and the Rockers.*

The End of the Golden Age

In America and Europe, the popularity of the scooter faded over the late 1960s and into the 1970s. By the mid-1970s, the scooter didn't hold the same cult status as in past decades. Scooters were looked upon as something to drive as a last resort. Also new environmental laws restricted the dirty two-stroke engines that most scooters used.

Just because Europeans and Americans were done playing with scooters didn't mean that the rest of the world was. By the mid-1970s, countries like India, Taiwan, and Japan had a growing need for cheap transportation. In India, a company called Scooters India bought Innocenti's design and improved it. Because of dense populations in eastern countries, there just wasn't space for big cars to roll down roads as in the United States. Scooters fit down narrow streets and could be parked anywhere. The necessity of cheap transportation kept the scooter alive yet again.

There are also strange reasons for people to drive scooters. People have used scooters in bullfights. The Toreadors would ride behind the driver, and hope that the scooter didn't stall when the bull was charging. Scooters were also used in an Ice Capades show. Some of the performers drove them around during a performance of Peter Pan. It must have been tricky to maneuver on ice with a boxy, clumsy scooter.

The group that was probably the best known for driving scooters were the Shriners. Often seen wearing fez caps and smiles, the Shriner Motor Corps would ride Cushman Eagles or Turtlebacks. They usually rode in Fourth of July parades, doing daredevil stunts and showing off their riding skills. Cushman made special accessories just for the Shriners. They could order special windshields, horns, Shriner flags, chrome extras, saddlebags, and even custom paint jobs.

Today people collect old scooters and restore them to their original condition. A growing crowd of people are willing to spend a lot of time and money on an old Vespa or Cushman. There are scooter clubs all over the world, dedicated to bringing back to life the golden age of the scooter. It's done all in the name of nostalgia. Companies are still making scooters, but not like those in the past. Honda makes a miniature version of its Gold Wing motorcycle, and Piaggio continues to make a Vespa-like scooter.

Countries with dense populations use scooters because there is not enough room on the roads for everyone to own a car.

Today's Scooters

A big problem with scooters is that they use a two-stroke engine, rather than a four-stroke engine like cars do. A two-stroke engine puts out a lot more pollution than a four-stroke. The pistons in a two stroke engine are lubricated with oil, therefore burning a lot of oil. This creates a lot of stinky exhaust. There are laws and high taxes on two-stroke engines in daily driving vehicles.

A lot of dirt bikes made for trail riding and racing have two-stroke engines also, but because they aren't used for daily driving, they don't pollute very much. Today, fortunately, governments and people are smarter about making the world a cleaner place to live. Scooter manufacturers are working on the two-stroke engine problem. A company called Unique Mobility is even working on an electric scooter.

In the future, scooters might look more like cars. The German car and motorcycle company, BMW, built a prototype of a scooter with a roll bar. The scooter would be safer to drive because the driver would be protected, yet still get the benefits of a scooter. Honda continues to make a more modern scooter design, and they can be seen on the roads today.

The scooters of today are much classier and come in a variety of models to fit everyone from densely populated countries to businessmen on the go.

A Scooter's Place in the World

Many things came out of the invention of the scooter. It led to the riding lawn mower, the golf cart, and product liability laws. After World War II, the scooter kept economies alive in Europe and Japan before four-wheeled transportation was easily available. Scooters were part of the reason that city people started visiting the country more often, and country people were able to frequent the city with regularity. The motorscooter was a tamed, less serious version of the motorcycle.

Everybody could use the lighter weight, slower machines. Women drove scooters more than motorcycles. During a time when it was considered unladylike to straddle a motorcycle, a scooter allowed for a woman driver to either stand or sit on her scooter.

The scooter made it possible for a woman to go out on her own with class. A woman on a scooter was more accepted than a woman on a motorcycle. Scooters gave women the freedom of movement and mobility. This new-found freedom and independence marked a new era for women around the world. Even the Queen of England was once transported on a scooter.

Scooters have helped soldiers across war-torn battlefields. They scooted women into more independent lives. They saw the rise and fall of the Mods. Scooters have had a great impact both economically and culturally in the world. Today, they are just plain fun and practical. If these high-styled mechanical oddballs managed to survive this long, the scooter is sure to be around for a long time to come.

Scooters have made many advances since the 1950s. The Honda Helix is a large scooter with lots of power and room.

Glossary

Bodywork - the outside covering on a motorcycle.

Clutch - connects the power from the engine to the rear wheel.

Cult Status - something that has cult status is highly regarded by a certain group of people.

Customize - to change or make better to a person's liking.

Depression - A time in history (1929-1940) when many people didn't have jobs and the economy was bad.

Four-Stroke Engine - a type of engine that uses valves to move gas inside the engine. It has a power stroke every fourth stroke of the piston.

Frivolous - not needed, extra, something just for fun.

Mileage - the amount of miles a scooter will go on a gallon of gas.

Nostalgia - a sentimental longing for something in the past.

Paratroopers - soldiers who parachuted from a plane to the ground.

Pistons - the part that moves up and down in the shaft of a cylinder.

Product Liability - a manufacturer taking responsibility for its product.

Steering Spindle - the rod that connects the steering wheel to the rest of the scooter.

Suspension - the system on a scooter that lifts the frame from the axle. Scooters often used springs for suspension.

Template - a pattern used as a guide to make many of the same thing.

Transmission - the system that transfers the power from the engine to the rear wheel.

Two-Stroke Engine - a type of engine that does not use valves to move gas inside the engine. It has a power stroke every second stroke of the piston.

Internet Sites

Minibike Central
http://www.geocities.com/MotorCity/7029/mini.html
This page shows pictures of awesome minibikes and tells how to make them. It also has plenty of photos of minibikes and minicycles. This site will give you information on where to find minibikes and parts.

Pete's SOLO Disabled Motorcycle Project
http://www.btinternet.com/~chaloner/pete/pete.htm
This website is about a different kind of custom bike. The page is for disabled people who want to ride a motorcycle. See photos of this customized bike, and how it works.

The Dirt Bike Pages
http://www.off-road.com/orcmoto.html
This site has action photos of all kinds of dirt bikes, monthly columns and articles, and product reports. This site has important riding information, too.

Scooter Magazine Online
http://www2.scootermag.it/scooter/
This web site is fully devoted to motorscooters. Technique, developments, new models, tests, and track and road trials.

The Motorcycle Database
http://www.motorcycle.informaat.nl/ehome.html
Over 250 motorcycles, their specifications and pictures, and driver experiences from visitors. Pick the model and year of motorcycle you would like to see. Photos and detailed information is included. Lots to see!

Pass It On

Motorcycle Enthusiasts: educate readers around the country by passing on information you've learned about motorcycles. Share your little-known facts and interesting stories. Tell others what your favorite kind of motorcycle is or what your favorite type of riding is. We want to hear from you!

To get posted on the ABDO & Daughters website E-mail us at "Sports@abdopub.com"

Visit the ABDO Publishing Company website at www.abdopub.com

Index